Hunting Neptune's Giants

Enjoy the hunt!
Catherine Gourley
Mystic, Ct
1955

HUNTING NEPTUNE'S GIANTS

True Stories of American Whaling

CATHERINE GOURLEY
IN ASSOCIATION WITH
MYSTIC SEAPORT MUSEUM

THE MILLBROOK PRESS
BROOKFIELD, CONNECTICUT

FOR DENNIS

Library of Congress Cataloging-in-Publication Data
Gourley, Catherine, 1950–
Hunting Neptune's giants : true stories of American whaling / by
Catherine Gourley; in association with Mystic Seaport Museum.
p.   cm.
Includes bibliographical references (p.   ) and index.
Summary: An account of American whaling using excerpts
from diaries, ships' logs, letters, and other documents written
by the men and women who participated in the industry
during the 19th century.
ISBN 1-56294-534-3
1. Whaling—United States—History—19th century—Juvenile
literature.   2. Whalers (Persons)—United States—History—19th
century—Juvenile literature.   3. Whalers (Persons)—United States—
Biography—Juvenile literature.   [1. Whaling—United States—
History—19th century.]   I. Mystic Seaport Museum.   II. Title.
SH383.2.G68   1995   639.2'8'0973—dc20   94-39993   CIP   AC

All photographs courtesy of the Mystic Seaport Museum

Contents

Hunting Neptune's Giants

The Prince of Whales

It was cold in Chicago in December of 1880. An icy wind gusted off Lake Michigan. But the freezing weather did not keep people away. Hundreds of curious men, women, and children stood in long lines outside the Exposition Building, waiting to enter and get a glimpse of "the monster."

For days, the Chicago newspapers had published stories about the monster. "Those seeking knowledge must see it," an advertising flyer said. "If you love your children, don't deny them the only opportunity they will ever have in their lives to see this MONARCH OF THE SEAS!"

Monster? Monarch? Just what lay inside Chicago's Exposition Building?

It was a show called The Prince of Whales. The prince was a frozen baleen whale nearly 60 feet (18 meters) long and weighing 72,000 pounds (32,000 kilograms). The advertisement was right. Very few people in America in 1880 had ever seen a real whale—living or dead. And unless they signed up on a three- or four-year whaling voyage, they probably would never see another.

The whale inside Chicago's Exposition Hall had been killed by a bomb lance in the North Atlantic Ocean a few months earlier. The bomb lance was a type of device used by American whalers in 1880. The lance entered the whale's body and then exploded. Ordinarily, the whale would have its blubber stripped and boiled into oil right there on the ship in the middle of the ocean. But this whale—the Prince of Whales—was not meant to be turned into oil to light lamps or lubricate machine parts. The Prince had a different destiny.

The man who had arranged for the whale's capture was George H. Newton, and he wanted the whale's body whole and undamaged. Newton was a businessman with a big idea. He was certain people would pay to see what they had never seen before—the largest creature on earth. His plan was to charge each adult twenty-five cents to see his whale. Children paid fifteen cents, and orphans a dime.

Once inside, the curious spectators walked slowly past the giant, which lay over two flat railroad cars. First, they saw its huge head and inside its open jaws the curtains of baleen that give the whale its name. Baleen consists of thin, bonelike strips. Baleen whales have it instead of teeth. It works like a strainer to trap krill, tiny ocean animals on which the whale feeds.

As the people moved down the line, they next saw the nostrils, called the blowhole, on top of the whale's head. A whale is not a fish. It is a mammal. It must come to the surface of the water to breathe. When it does, it exhales a fountain of warm vapor through its blowhole and takes in fresh air.

Perched on top of the Prince of Whales was Captain McCarthy. He wasn't a real whaling captain. He was an actor hired by George Newton. As the people filed past the frozen carcass, McCarthy spouted interesting tidbits about whales and the men who hunted them. He would have explained that the baleen whale was also called the right whale, because it did not sink when it died. That was why it was the *right* whale to hunt.

Pointing to the monster's tiny eyes, he could have told the crowd that a whale's eyes often wept greasy tears. Or he might have explained how, when struck with a harpoon, a frightened whale's first instinct is to flee, not to fight.

And then, inching his way along the whale's black hide, Captain McCarthy would point to the Prince's flukes. Its monster tail was 7 feet (2 meters) long and more than 12 feet (over 3 meters) wide. These flukes could smash a whaleboat into splinters, and sometimes did.

Newton's whale show was a huge success. Each night after closing the exhibit at 10:00 P.M., he went back to his hotel room alone to count up the thousands of nickels, dimes, and quarters he had collected during the day. He had only one worry: there was no refrigeration in 1880. Still, as long as the weather stayed cold, the show could go on. And it did.

At the end of January, Newton covered the carcass with canvas and ice and headed north to Milwaukee, Wisconsin. A few weeks later, he and his monster cruised by rail to St. Louis, then to Cincinnati and Pittsburgh and Philadelphia. The Prince of Whales had become a traveling circus.

Then came the spring thaw. The Prince began to stink. People no longer needed newspaper advertisements to learn of the whale's arrival. They could smell it. When efforts to mummify the rotting carcass failed, Newton went out of business. His whale show, like the mighty Prince himself, had gone belly-up.

The American whaling industry in the 1880s was also showing signs of dying. For more than 200 years, whales like the Prince were hunted. Their baleen, or whalebone, was shaped into buggy whips and fishing rods, ladies' girdles and skirt hoops. The oil from their blubber was used to light lamps, to prepare leather, and to oil machine parts. Other kinds of whales, sperm whales, were also hunted for spermaceti and ambergris. Spermaceti is an oily substance stored in the whale's head. It was used to make odorless and clean-burning candles. Ambergris is a black and waxy substance formed in the whale's intestines. It was used in making perfumes and other cosmetics. Whalebone, oil, and ambergris helped America grow into an independent and prosperous country. Products that weren't used by Americans at home were sold to other countries for a profit.

With the success of whaling, other businesses boomed onshore as well. Workers made rope for harpoons and the ships' rigging, and wooden barrels to hold the oil. Sail makers turned canvas into sails. Just as George Newton counted his money after each show, owners of whaling ships and onshore factories counted their profits after each voyage. Whaling made some Americans very rich.

But by the 1880s another oil, called petroleum, had been discovered in Pennsylvania, and people were turning away from whale oil as a source of light. Whales were becoming scarce. Whaling ships stayed at sea for long stretches of time—four or even five years—before taking enough whales to fill all the barrels in a ship's hold. Profits were dropping and, with them, America's interest in whaling. Still, the whalers hung on into the 1900s. When the *Wanderer*, one of the last wooden whaleships, wrecked on the rocks off Cuttyhunk, Massachusetts, in 1924, an important chapter in America's history ended.

George H. Newton's whale show was a short-lived curiosity. The true story of American whaling could never be told by a phony sea captain perched on top of a rotting whale carcass. The true story of the hunt for bone and oil is best told by the hunters themselves. They are the ones who planted the barbed harpoons in the whale's hide and were towed by the frightened animal until it could flee no more. They are the ones who twisted the lance deeper into the whale's back until dark clots of blood sprayed from its blowhole. And when at last the whale rolled on its side and turned fin out—dead—it was the hunters who towed the floating carcass back to the ship. There, as sharks circled in the bloody water, the men cut off the whale's head and stripped away blankets of blubber, then boiled the blubber in pots on the ship's deck.

Many of the men, and a number of the women who went whaling with them, wrote about their lives at sea in letters and logbooks and journals that they kept during their long voyages. They wrote about their fears and loneliness so far from home. They wrote about the thrill of the hunt and the back-breaking work on deck cutting up the whale and boiling it down. They wrote about floggings and mutinies, cannibals and hurricanes. Many of their stories have been saved in maritime libraries, like the G. W. Blunt White Library at the Mystic Seaport Muscum in Mystic, Connecticut. Some stories are still being discovered in musty notebooks in sea chests long forgotten in attics and cellars.

The true story of American whaling lives on in the voices of these hunters. By gathering excerpts from diaries, letters, ships' logs, and other documents, this book captures those voices and lets them speak for themselves of what it was like to hunt Neptune's giants.

We have but one man before the mast that was ever whaling, Ethan Topping, but our anticipation is very great. At 10 P.M. we lose sight of our native land and steer off to the southeast into a pathless ocean.

Henry Green

To the Ocean Pasture: The Crews

Americans were not the first whalers. Drawings carved into cave walls in Norway show that creatures from the sea, including dolphins and whales, were being hunted thousands of years ago. It is believed that Norse hunters used small boats to drive the whales into shallow bays where they could kill them and then haul the carcasses onto shore.

The Basques, people who lived near the Bay of Biscay between France and Spain, began to hunt whales with harpoons and lines nearly one thousand years ago. People who lived in other parts of the world also hunted whales, using the meat for food and the whale oil for heating. In America as early as 1650, Puritans who lived on Cape Cod, Massachusetts, and Long Island, New York, killed whales from shore and sold the oil and bone. Within fifty years, however, Americans would change whaling forever by hunting not from shore but in the deeper oceans. In doing so, they would organize the hunt into one of the world's largest—and bloodiest—money-making industries.

This expansion of the American whaling industry began in 1690 on a small island called Nantucket in the North Atlantic Ocean off the coast of Massachusetts. Native Indians and Quaker settlers lived on the island. One day, so the story goes, some Quakers were standing high on a hill when they saw whales offshore spouting and swimming. One man pointed. "There," he predicted, "is a green pasture where our children's grandchildren will go for bread."

What he meant was that the huge mammals were a rich natural resource, there for the taking. The Quakers of Nantucket, who hated violence and thought it was a sin to take another human life, looked to the sea as a pasture to harvest. No one knows for sure just who this man was, but within twenty years his prediction had come true. The American whaling industry had begun to grow and prosper.

For the first one hundred years of American whaling, the crews were mostly young American men—Quakers and Indians from Nantucket, farm boys from New York, Massachusetts, and Pennsylvania. They had many reasons for becoming whalemen.

Adventure

Many went for adventure. Whaling meant the chance to travel to exotic ports in South America or unknown islands in the South Pacific. It also presented a thrilling opportunity to hunt an awesome creature. Still others had just emerged from boyhood and were eager to prove themselves in a dangerous, difficult job.

Nelson Cole Haley

Nelson Cole Haley was just seventeen when he signed up as a boatsteerer on the *Charles W. Morgan*. A boatsteerer's job was to plant

The ship Nelson Cole Haley sailed on, the *Charles W. Morgan*. Sailors work in the ship's rigging and look out for whales from high in its mastheads.

the harpoon in the back of the whale. Haley almost didn't get the job. First, he had to convince the ship's owner, a man called Black Hawk Robinson, that he was man enough to dart a harpoon. Haley later wrote a book called *Whale Hunt* about his adventures on the *Charles W. Morgan*. Included in the book is this scene, Haley's first encounter with Black Hawk.

> The Captain went into Mr. Robinson's office with me when I went to sign the shipping papers. I found him to be a tall man (six feet [1.8 meters] at least) with keen black eyes and a hawkbill nose, with a very dark complexion. I then saw why he was nicknamed "Black Hawk." He arose and shook hands with the Captain; and looking down on me with his eagle eyes, he said, "The ship you want to sail in can command the very smartest men for officers and boatsteerers. . . . You look young and small for the position you would have to fill on board that ship."
>
> I felt a little embarrassed (I was but seventeen years old, and stood but little over five feet [1.5 meters] in height) and hardly knew what to say. Turning to the Captain, he said, "You pick your own men, and if he will suit you for a boatsteerer it is all right." The Captain told him it was. Then he turned to me again and said, "Do you think you could strike a whale?"
>
> I told him I had struck sharks and dolphins; and that whales were so much larger, I thought I could if the boat I steered got near enough to one. He looked at me a minute with twinkling eyes and replied, "Well, often valuable articles are in small parcels."

Haley's voyage on the *Charles W. Morgan* was not his first time at sea. But many men who signed up for whaling voyages had never before set foot on a ship's deck. They were called greenhands.

These inexperienced sailors knew nothing about the miserable living conditions, the rough treatment by the officers, or the hard work expected of them. Nor did they realize how little money they could receive for all their sweat and suffering.

Ambition

Still, whaling sounded like a good deal. Once the whaleship returned home, each crew member received a percentage of the profits from the sale of bone and oil to merchants. This was the lay system, and it drew ambitious young men from land.

But what many greenhands did not know was that throughout the voyage the captain kept a careful record for each man and deducted amounts from his share, or lay, of the profits. If the weather turned frigid and a man needed to buy an extra blanket from the ship's stores, that was a deduction. If he needed to borrow from his lay in advance, while in a foreign port, that was also deducted from his final wage. By the end of the voyage, some men ended up owing the ship's owners money. The common way to work off the debt was to agree to go to sea again.

Henry Green

Greenhands like Henry Green received the smallest lay, while the officers and the captain received the largest. In 1817, Green's wage for twelve months and twelve days at sea on board the *Fair Helen* was $135.27½ cents—or about 35 cents per day. But Green was not discouraged. He went whaling again. Over the next four voyages, he quickly advanced from boatsteerer to mate. With each promotion, his earnings grew. Then, in 1821, he found himself learning all over again, this time in the position of captain. He wrote about his new responsibility in a diary he kept during the voyage.

> This is the first voyage that ever I took charge of. I am very young at the business and my ship very old. I am 26½ years old. The ship is 79. My officers and crew have had as little experience as myself. I have but two men *before the mast** that have ever been more than one voyage at sea. . . . [But] If there are any right whales living, we will get some.

At the end of this voyage, Green's earnings amounted to more than $2,000.

> I have made a living of it and not much more but I am determined to follow the business with hopes of making something in time. It is hard for a man to whale all his life and die poor at last. The business is by no means agreeable much more the dangers that we are exposed to, but some men would go to the sea for money.

Escape and Kidnapping

Nelson Cole Haley and Henry Green signed on for their voyages because they were ambitious. But others went whaling for very different reasons. For some American blacks who were hired to crew a ship, whaling became a means of freeing themselves from slavery. Still other men were forced into the industry, like slaves.

Prince Boston and Black Man Mariner

The Quakers who lived on Nantucket did not approve of slavery. Still, some people on the island owned black slaves. John Swain was one of those people. Among his slaves was a man named Prince Boston. In 1769, Boston escaped from his owner by signing

*Italicized terms through-out the book will be defined in the margin.

in the forward part of the ship where deck hands live

aboard the whaler *Friendship*, which was owned by William Rotch. It is likely Rotch knew that Boston was a runaway slave and didn't care.

When the ship returned to Nantucket, Rotch ordered the captain to pay Boston his lay of the profits. Then John Swain appeared. He not only demanded that Boston be returned to him as his personal property, but also sued Rotch for the money Boston had earned while at sea. The case went to court. In keeping with the Quaker belief that no person should be enslaved by another, the jury ruled in favor of Rotch. But the court didn't stop there. It declared Prince Boston a free man.

Prince Boston was one of many black men to sail on a whaler. But his courtroom victory on Nantucket opened the way for many more Africans and African Americans to earn their living as free men. By the early 1800s about one third of all Nantucket's whalemen were black.

Prince Boston's grandson, Absalom, became one of the few black whaling captains. He was known as "Black Man Mariner." His ship was the *Industry*. In 1822, at a time when many blacks in America were trapped in a life of slavery, Absalom sailed from Nantucket with an entirely black crew.

Around the mid-1800s, however, whaling crews began to change. Low wages, filthy living conditions, and even longer voyages made it more difficult for whaling agents to sign up crews. The farm boys could earn more money elsewhere. And the sea was no longer the only avenue of adventure. Another had opened up— the American West.

And yet there were still some men who would go whaling—men with ambition, men seeking adventure, but also men who needed a place to hide out a while. Thugs, convicts, and drunkards began to fill the ships now. In addition, captains began recruiting men from foreign ports to crew the American whaleships.

Roderick Corvello

Roderick Corvello was Portuguese. He grew up in the Azores, a chain of islands in the Atlantic Ocean off the coast of Portugal. The Azores were often the first stop for a whaling ship on its journey. Here the captain recruited hogs, wood, and vegetables—and, Corvello remembered, additional men.

> Boats would need more crew sometimes and, to get them, they would go around to bars. Men would be brought back to the ship and then they'd wake up. Others were criminals. They could choose to go to jail or go to sea. The best men were the ones they picked up from the Cape Verdes and the Azores. They were no trouble at all.

A Multicultural Industry

American whaling was an industry of many nationalities and races—Americans, African Americans, Portuguese from the Azores and Cape Verde Islands, West Indians from the Caribbean islands, and Polynesians—called Kanackers—from the islands in the South Pacific.

Although their faces and skin colors were different, their motivations for signing aboard whalers were similar. Some followed adventure. Others sought ambition. And still others longed for freedom, escaping from one country to another on a whaler.

The whaling schooner, the *Margarett,* was manned
by a crew of many races and ethnic backgrounds
and many levels of experience and expertise.

Once cramped aboard the ship, the cultures and languages of these men often clashed. Whaling masters had prejudices about the different groups. For example, some captains thought the Portuguese were hard workers who followed orders without questions. If a mate or captain showed favoritism to a "Gee" because of this, then a brawl among the men might explode later below deck.

But once the hunt was on and the chase after a whale begun, the whalemen spoke a common language. Skin color was often forgotten, and a man was judged by his courage, strength, and quick thinking on the sea.

Daily Life

No matter what kinds of men made up the crew, the harsh realities of daily life aboard a whaler set in once the ship lifted anchor. Greenhands, in particular, suffered from seasickness caused by the endless pitch and roll of the ship.

Sixteen-year-old Nathaniel Morgan wrote in his diary soon after the *Hannibal* left New London, Connecticut, ". . . unpleasant, cold and rainy—begin to disrelish [dislike] the smell of food." Elizabeth Stetson, whose husband was captain of the *Rosa Baker*, summarized her first seasick weeks aboard this way: "Eat and then vomit is the order of the day."

In time, both Morgan and Stetson overcame their seasickness, but other hardships made daily life a challenge.

Crossing the Line

During the first weeks of traveling to the whaling grounds, the experienced mates worked the new men hard. The green crew practiced lowering the whaleboats used for chasing the prey. They toughened the skin of their hands and the muscles in their backs rowing for hours over the ocean. They attacked dummy whales—bobbing barrels that had been thrown overboard. They learned the names of each sail and how to trim, or adjust, the sails so that the snapping canvas caught the full breath of the wind and drove the ship forward. They got over any fear of heights they might have had by climbing the rigging to the masthead, or lookout post, high above the deck.

By the time the ship crossed the equator, or the "line," the greenhands were no longer green and were anxious now to take their first whale. That's when rumors of a visit from Old Neptune, the Roman god of the ocean, began to swirl about the ship.

Nathaniel Morgan

33 degrees; side of ship's forward end protected from wind

Nat Morgan was sixteen when he crossed the line for the first time on the *Hannibal*. The ceremony that marked his passage from greenhand to sailor was a tradition on many whalers.

About 7 in the evening the lookout at the masthead sung out "Sail ho."

"Where away?" asked the officer of the deck.

"Three points off the *lee bow."*

"What does she look like?"

"A low black schooner."

All the greenhands were ordered below, and soon after the ship was hailed in a rough voice—"Ship ahoy."

"Hallo."

"What ship is that?"

"The *Hannibal* of New London."

"Are any of my children aboard?"

"Yes—a few—come aboard."

Old Neptune then came on board. . . . There was a tremendous trampling on deck amidst the rattling of chains and rigging. "Let me see some of my children," says the old veteran god of the waters.

The boys were then taken out of the *forecastle*, one by one, I being the fourth child it would seem on this majesty program. I was taken on deck—blindfolded and led along into the *waist* and placed upon a seat. Old father Neptune I could not see, but could hear him all round, and he seemed in most excellent spirits. I was asked a number of questions . . . which I answered with all due respect. The ceremonies were accompanied by various kinds of instrumental music, one instrument being an old piece of an iron hoop drawn across the *chine* of an empty water cask.

After the questions were finished and satisfactorily answered, I was ordered to be shaved. Accordingly, I was lathered with a *patent* chemical soap, compounded of tar and *slush*, and then most delightfully shaved with this same identical musical iron hoop *Eolean* razor. Then, at the word, "rinse him," I found myself suddenly ducked backwards into the deck tub full of water.

Old Neptune then informed me that I was initiated regularly, and could be a spectator of the remaining ceremonies. The other greenhands were shaved pretty much in the same manner, and after all had been initiated the whole crew and officers had a regular time of throwing buckets of water at each other. Those who were not soaked through were scarce, and I think Old Nep himself for once got as much salt water as he wanted.

section of ship before the mast where men lived

middle of ship

edge

commercial leftover cooking grease

musical

Living Conditions

To some, a whaler was an ugly lump of a ship. Measuring an average length of just over 100 feet (30 meters), a whaler was wide, heavy, and—compared with other sleeker ships—a slow sailer.

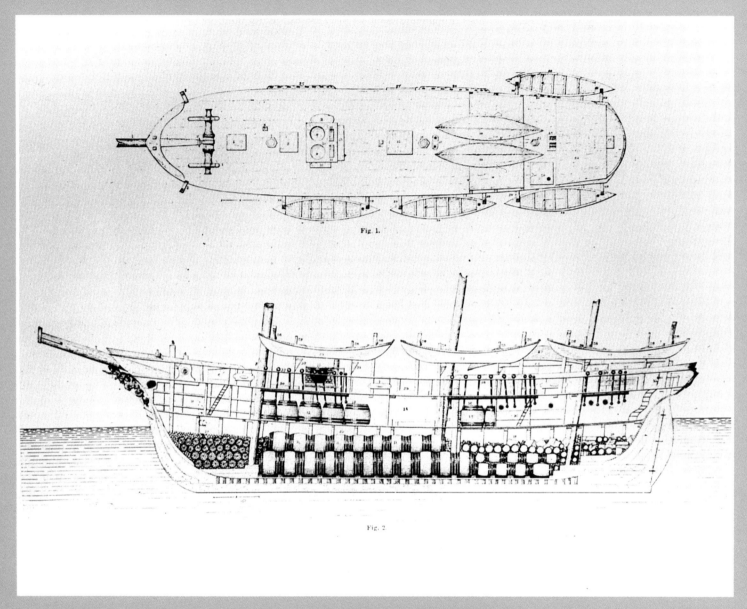

Fig. 1.

Fig. 2

Robert Cushman Murphy, whose words are recorded in the next chapter, drew this cross-section of his ship, the *Daisy*. Much of the whaler's space was set aside for barrels of oil, leaving little room for living quarters.

The wide body allowed for plenty of storage space in the hold for hundreds of barrels of whale oil. A whaler didn't have to be fast to get its job done. It cruised the oceans, migrating with the whales north, then south, then north again.

For years at a time, approximately thirty men and sometimes a woman and children—the family of the captain—shared the whaler's cramped quarters. The captain's living quarters included a private bedroom and an after cabin. No one, not even his officers, could enter the after cabin without the captain's permission.

The main cabin was a dining area that also served as a meeting room. The captain shared this space with his mates, or officers. The mates slept in tight quarters off this main room.

Beyond this area was the steerage section of the ship. Here boat-steerers like Nelson Cole Haley lived. Here also slept the cooper, whose job it was to hammer together the casks that held the oil; the carpenter; and sometimes the cook and the cabin boy.

John A. States

John A. States held none of these positions. He was not captain, nor mate, nor boatsteerer, nor cooper. At eighteen, he had signed on the whaler *Eugene* as a common seaman. His berth, or bunk, was in a crowded, dark space called the forecastle, which he shared with sixteen to twenty other men. The forecastle was in front of the foremast, where the roll and pitch of the ship in the ocean was more keenly felt. Here the bunks were two and three deep. A string could be nailed from one end to the other end of the bunk and a cloth hung over it for a curtain. That was all the privacy there was to be had. Nor did the forecastle have windows or fresh air. The smell of bilge water, tobacco smoke, and men's sweat hung thick in the air.

The captain and mates went below to their quarters through the companionway. This was a narrow stair at the rear of the ship. It was forbidden for common seamen like John States to use the companionway or go anywhere below deck aft, or after the mast. The way into and out of the forecastle was through a hatch through the foredeck. A ladder led down into the smoky hole that was the seamen's home.

States spent a good part of his three-year whaling voyage in the forecastle. In his journal he described what a typical morning in the forecastle was like.

> By the dim light of the lamp which is swinging to and fro in the gloomy forecastle may be seen a group of sleepers who, worn out with fatigue and watching, are now enjoying a few moments of troubled rest. . . . Yonder lies four of that class of persons to whom a little money is a fortune and who are striving to amass enough to carry them [back] to their native country.
>
> *rank*
>
> . . . Beneath one of these sleeps a toil worn sailor. Left an orphan in his early years when he most needed the comforting hand of a parent, he has struggled through the world to earn a scanty pittance. . . . Beneath him is one who has left his home a boy and who has now grown to a man's *estate*. . . . There is yet another who does not partake of even the pleasure of dreaming. He who is laid upon the bed of sickness awake and in pain. To him the hours pass slowly and drearily away.
>
> . . . Time rolls along and the sleepers still continue their slumbers. When bursting upon the ear comes the hoarse notes of the

summons for them to rise and renew their toil after perhaps four hours sleep. Slowly they rise, their sweet dreams dissipated and themselves awake to the sad reality. Now they commence their preparations for their morning meal. Out from their corners they bring their tin pots and pans and seating themselves around upon their chests, each facing his *messmates*, await the coming of their meal. Soon it comes, a bucket full of boiled coffee without molasses, a scanty supply of salt beef with hard, wormy bread constitutes their meal and of this, bad as it is, they have not enough.

crewmen who shared a meal

Salt Junk and Hardtack

The beef that John States and countless other sailors ate was sometimes called salt junk. The beef was packed in a barrel of salt to keep it from decaying during months at sea. Sometimes the salt worked. Sometimes it didn't. "June 28. Had to heave one barrel of meat overboard," wrote William Tallman on board the *London Packet.* "It had turned black and green and almost every other color but it stunk (also) enough to knock a man down 150 yards."

Whalers also ate hardtack, a type of hard, dry cracker made of flour. But at times even the barrels of flour could be spoiled—with bugs. Weevils, maggots, and cockroaches all wormed their way into the barrels stowed in the ship's hold. But instead of heaving the infested flour overboard, the cook fried or baked the weevils right into the bread. Men dunked their hardtack into their mugs of hot coffee, then skimmed the scalded bugs off the top before drinking.

Salt beef or salt pork, hardtack, and coffee sweetened with molasses was the common menu for the men in the forecastle, day after day. Beans, sweet potatoes when they were available, and rice were also served up. The only breaks in the monotony of the menu came once or twice a week when the cook served duff, a boiled pudding made with raisins, much like a fruit cake, or when one of the men managed to capture something fresh from the sea.

Francis Olmstead

Incidents of a Whaling Voyage is the title of a book written by Francis Olmstead soon after he returned from a voyage on the whaler *North America*. In the book, he described a tasty sea treat.

break

tried to bite

> We have taken several fine turtles within a few days, weighing from fifty to eighty pounds each, which made a very pleasant *interlude* in our accustomed fare. These turtles exhibited a most remarkable tenacity of life. . . . Their heads, as they lay upon deck, for more than half an hour after being severed from their bodies, *laid hold* of whatever touched them, with convulsive energy, while their eyes glared wildly every few minutes.

Olmstead and the crew also looked forward to another favorite food: doughnuts fried in the clear oil taken from the head of a sperm whale. On the *North America* and hundreds of other whalers, this special treat was a celebration, served only after 1,000 barrels of whale oil had been stowed below.

Whaleman Robert Weir described a different sea treat: barnacles scraped from the noses of slaughtered right whales. This crust of parasites was called the whale's "bonnet." In his journal, Weir wrote, "The barnacles are enormous, as much as two inches deep—the boys often roast them and eat them the same as oysters."

Captain Samuel Braley

In the beginning months of a voyage, most whaleships carried livestock boarded in pens on deck. The chickens and hogs were meant to feed the captain and his mates, especially when they entertained officers from another ship during a gam, or visit. But one captain, at least, kept a pig as a pet. When the pig died, he wrote a poem about it in his journal.

> My darling Pigy's back was broke:
> For fear that she might suffer;
> I kindly cut her little throat
> And had her fried for supper.

Charlie Stetson

A parrot was a more common pet aboard ship, but fourteen-year-old Charlie Stetson, the son of Elizabeth and Captain Stetson, had both a monkey and a dog during his voyage on the *Rosa Baker*. Charlie and the two animals played together. But the deck of a whaleship could be a dangerous playground, even for animals. "Shag the dog fell overboard this afternoon," Charlie wrote in his journal. "Lowered a boat and got him. Brought him aboard. He was in the water about 5 min."

Then there were the rats.

Lilian Baker Fenton

Lilian Fenton was a whaling wife. Life was somewhat better for women who went whaling with their husbands, the captains. The women were confined, just as the forecastle hands were, to certain sections of the ship, both above deck and below. A wife lived aft in the captain's cabin and parlor, but she shared meals with the

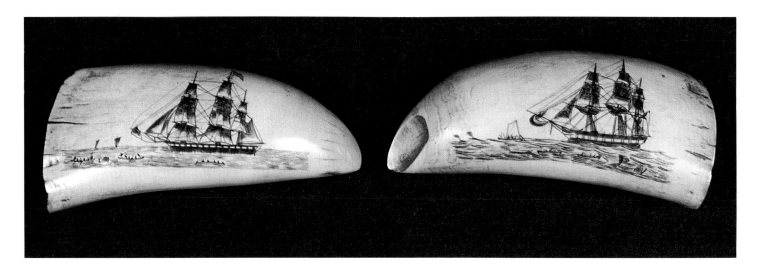

Classic whaling scenes carved on sperm whale teeth. The first tooth shows an overturned whaleboat. The second tooth clearly shows a whale-boat's sailing rig.

officers in the main cabin. When there were no whales to chase or cut up, the men filled the long hours with tedious ship duties. In their free time, some carved designs on whalebone or sculpted the bone into cane handles and other decorative objects. The process was called scrimshawing. But the captain's wife had no official ship's duties. She might fill her days by sewing clothes, ironing, or caring for the sick. She rarely cooked. Mostly she read or, like Lilian Baker Fenton, wrote in her journal.

This excerpt taken from Fenton's journal, which she kept during the cruise of the *Ohio* from 1858 to 1862, may be an exaggeration or even a sea yarn. Perhaps she recorded it because she found it

The 1864 wedding portrait of Nelson Cole Haley, whose words appear in this book, and his wife, Charlotte Brown Haley.

amusing. Whatever the case, rats were almost always found on whaleships.

> Day after day, [the] cook complained that eggs were disappearing. [The captain], having an idea that cook himself had a fondness for eggs paid no attention. One day the captain lay on a couch, his head aching badly. He dozed and was awakened by a little noise. . . . what he saw was startling. Along the floor moved slowly a strange procession. A large rat lay on his back, his four legs grasping securely one egg! Another rat was dragging him carefully by the tail back to their own *larder*.

pantry

Also aboard the *Ohio* during this cruise was Captain Fenton's seven-year-old son, Willie. Children of whaling captains, like Willie Fenton and Charlie Stetson, sometimes lived aboard ship with their father and mother. For other children, their fathers were strangers because they were away at sea so long. Going on a whaling voyage, however, made it possible for the family to be together. Lilian Fenton described her son's awe and excitement the day he was taken aboard the *Ohio*.

> Young Willie was so excited he couldn't keep still, but tried to see everything on the ship in the first 15 min. His eyes popped with the wonder of living four years in such a small place.

Being at sea, however, did not mean a vacation from schoolwork or chores. Many children spent hours below deck reading and practicing their arithmetic. Other lessons were on deck without a book or slate tablet. Charlie Stetson, for example, learned how to harpoon sharks. And his father often took Charlie with him in the whaleboats. "Father lowered the boats to learn the greenhands how to pull," wrote Charlie in his journal, pages of which are filled with handwriting exercises. "He says I may go in the boats by and by." Captain Stetson also taught his son how to read the stars to determine the exact location of the ship on the pathless ocean.

Willie Fenton learned a different lesson—how to swim. His father tied a rope around Willie and lowered him into the ocean. Although the child was terrified, he knew he must obey his father just as all the other men on board ship obeyed him. His mother was also frightened and wept while she watched the swimming lesson. But, she wrote later in her journal, the captain's method had worked—Willie learned how to swim.

Bathing

Keeping clean on board a whaleship was no more pleasant than dining. Water for bathing could not be spared. But the men had a unique method for removing the stinking residue of whale oil and blood from their clothes.

Harry Chippendale

The son of a whaling captain, Harry Chippendale was born at sea on the *Alice Knowles* in 1879. At sixteen, he returned to the sea as a whaleman. In his book *Sails and Whales* he explained how the sailors washed their clothes.

drain hole

> Unless rain water was collected, which was not very often, water for washing clothes had to be tapped from the "head," a barrel with holes drilled in one end and used as a urinal by the men. Whenever water for washing was needed, the "head" was tapped at the *bung*. I did not enter into that procedure very willingly at first, but I had

accepting no alternative, and after a while I became *reconciled,* as the garments were tied to the end of a line and towed for two or three days in the briny ocean, then brought aboard and hung out to dry, resulting in a wash that was spotlessly clean and free from odor of any sort. In fact, I soon found out that was the only possible way to remove the greasy whale oil from our clothing.

"Shamefully Deceived"

To many, the experience of daily life aboard a whaler proved what was often said of whaling, that it was one notch above slavery. Any illusions men harbored about the profession were quickly smashed after time on the open sea.

William H. Woods

William H. Woods, seventeen, wrote letters home. In this one to his friend Moses Pearson, he summed up his whaling life. At the time, Woods was cruising somewhere off the west coast of Africa on the bark *President.*

At Sea May 26, 1878

Well Mose,

I have now got an opportunity to write you a few lines to let you know that I am alive and kicking hoping this letter will find you the same way. I am a lucky dog to feel all right for the first whale I *attacked* *went on* came very near fixing the whole boats crew. We came as near death as I want to go. The way the old whale kicked round was a caution to us. He turned the boat bottom side up and of course we could not get out of his way so he had us at his mercy but no one got hurt. The second mate took our line and we made out to save the whale. The worst part of it was we had nothing to eat from seven o'clock till twelve that night and working hard all day and night too. If you know when you are well off you will stay on land but if you should ever feel like going to sea take my advice and not come whaling but go on a merchant ship or a coaster. There you are in port quite often but on a whaler you have to stay out at sea seven or eight months at a time and another thing you never make any thing the first voyage. Now you wait till you get to be an officer then you will not only get money fast but good grub while the poor fellows fore the mast get nothing but salt junk and hardtack and I can tell you that the meat does not always smell the best. 50 dollars would not hire you to take a bit of it at home. I have seen the hardtack crawl two feet away from the fellows that were eating it, it was so full of maggots and meat the same and I don't think you care much about eating live food if you don't you had better stay away from whaling.

from your old chum
Will Woods

John A. States

John States greeted the year 1846 from his sickbed, his narrow bunk in the dark forecastle of the *Nantasket.* Like Elizabeth Stetson and Will Woods, States wrote in his journal about his disappointment in this hard whaling life.

type of whaler

Jan. 1. New Year's Day and a contrast to the last then full of hope and joyful anticipation. . . . Instead of friends and schoolmates I find myself among strangers stretched on a bed of sickness. Here I am now in my berth writing for occupation in dreadful pain in the most discouraging circumstances with an aching heart. The dawning of last New Year's Day saw me in the old *barque*'s forecastle and confidently looking forward to the time when I should exchange that situation for a better one. Then the sight of a whale sent a thrill of pleasure to my heart for I saw before me an opportunity of distinguishing myself and a prospect of rising in my profession . . .

I consider that I have been shamefully deceived. . . . the sight of a whale now fills my mind with the most disagreeable feelings. . . . However, it will all be right if I can only get home.

Getting home was not likely to happen soon. The captain of the *Nantasket* was unhappy with the small amount of oil his crew had taken. The rumor that the ship would stay at sea another season proved true. The captain ordered a change of course, and the *Nantasket* headed for the North Pacific and another year of whaling.

Home for John States was still thousands of miles and at least another year away.

He rolled over and we went up to him again and soon killed him without raising his flukes out of the water, and lucky for us he didn't.

Smith Leek

Discipline, Danger, and Death

In addition to the hardships of daily life, men and women aboard whalers faced other perils: tyrannical captains, rough weather, and incurable illnesses. A whaling voyage could become a struggle for survival at sea, a struggle that some lost.

A Taste of the Cat

On a whaleship, all men were not created equal. The captain held absolute authority. His word was law on board. If a sailor resisted the back-breaking work, refused to take a watch, or challenged the authority of the captain or officers in some way, the sailor would be disciplined. The captain might order him to be confined to his berth in the forecastle for a time, to be chained in irons, or to be flogged.

Floggings were usually carried out in front of the other crew members so that they might learn by example not to disobey an officer. An officer could have a man tied by his thumbs in the rigging so that only the tips of his toes touched the deck or have him tied securely to a rail or grate. Then the man's back was

Flogging, a "taste of the cat," is shown in this lithograph. Notice how the other crew members turn away.

stripped bare. As the rest of the crew watched, the designated officer or the captain himself would cut loose with the cat. The cat was a leather rope or whip with multiple tails, each knotted on the end. The first lash almost always broke open the skin. The second and third strikes deepened the wounds. By the tenth or fourteenth strike, a man's back was raw and bloody.

Captain Shuman Gray

Shuman L. Gray was master of the *Hannibal*, the ship on which Nat Morgan sailed. Gray was an abusive captain. His foul language shocked Morgan. Worse were the seemingly impulsive beatings he gave to the hands. Whenever Morgan wrote about these beatings in his journal, he credited the information to a man named Dan. Dan was Dan E. Way, a boatsteerer on the *Hannibal* and Morgan's friend. Perhaps Morgan thought it safer to attribute his reports of the captain's violence to someone else. Whatever the reason, it seemed that Morgan and Dan discussed the captain's treatment of the crew and disapproved of it.

> Dan writes in his journal "between 4 and 6 P.M. the capt. kicked and pounded John Bull (a Kanacker) at the wheel so that he can scarcely move, and cannot turn himself in his berth—this is not the first man he has pounded at the wheel and the worst and most profane language I ever heard from mortal lips flows from his—"
> I think ditto.

*   *   *

> Dan says in his journal . . . of today—"At 6½ P.M. the capt. beat John Bull the Kanacker again at the wheel with a piece of rope until his body was all covered with ridges—this is the 3rd time he

has beat this man at the wheel—once laying him up for several
days—Is there no law? No friend? No justice to *redress* his wrongs?
Or must he receive the most brutal treatment from a tyrannical
shipmaster, and because he is ignorant of the language and laws of
the country, can have no redress—It is my determination now, to
lay these *aggravated* cases before a just court on our return, and see
if the sufferer can get no redress.

remedy

serious

In 1850 while the *Hannibal* was at sea, the United States passed a
law abolishing floggings on vessels of commerce. It is unlikely that
Captain Gray knew of the law before the ship returned to port. But
even if he had, he might not have cared. The beatings continued
on the *Hannibal*.

At 5 P.M., the 3rd mate gave Thomas, one of the Portuguese,
several blows in the face and kicked him, bruising him badly and
making his nose bleed. The capt. then took it up and continued
the beating and kicking. Then lashed him up to the *starboard* rail
and gave him 8 solid blows with a piece of *rattling*. The man then
said something which I could not hear, upon which the capt. dou-
bled the rattling making 4 parts to it and gave him 7 blows more as
hard as he could lay on. After a little time, he untied him. The
man came forward and set down on the *booby hatch* and cried so
loud that he started the men up from below. Goldsmith then exam-
ined him and found his back from his shoulders to his hips covered
with ridges and raw places. He called Nathaniel Morgan to witness
his back.

right side

strap

covered hole

The journal stops at the end of the voyage and so it is not clear
whether Way or anyone else ever brought charges against Captain

Gray. But this much is known. Years later, Morgan distinguished himself as an officer in the United States Navy during the Civil War. As for Captain Gray, he continued to master whaling vessels for twenty years more. Then, in 1868, he met a sour end. He died during a voyage. His wife was traveling with him. Rather than bury her husband at sea, she ordered his body placed inside a barrel of whiskey.

And there the pickled Shuman Gray remained until his ship returned home again.

Bury Me Not in the Deep, Deep Sea

Quinton Degrasse

Death was a passenger on all whaleships. Sometimes it came slowly and quietly, infecting the body with chickenpox, smallpox, or fever. Other times death thundered quickly out of a dark sea or sky.

The *Alice Knowles* was one of the last of the wooden whaleships. It sailed from New Bedford, Massachusetts, on April 9, 1915 and never returned. A hurricane destroyed it and all but two members of the crew. The storm began with a water spout, a spinning, funnel-shaped cloud like a sea-borne tornado. Quinton Degrasse was one of the two survivors. He had signed on for the four-year whaling voyage when the ship stopped at St. Vincent in the Cape Verde Islands to take on supplies and additional men. It was his first cruise on a whaleship and his first time leaving home. He was seventeen.

The guy on the lookout up in the mast thought he saw a whale spouting off. Then he said, "It ain't no whale, it's a water spout!"

The clouds turned black. The wind picked up and the rain started pouring as we took down the sails. But it did no good because the waves were so high that they smashed the boat.

In the last moments, Captain Hegarty grabbed hold of my hand and said, "Tough luck!" I said, "We're all in tough luck." We weren't able to hold onto each other. The boat rose on a wave . . . dropped over the crest, and shattered.

I hit my head against the boat but kept swimming until I found half of a whale boat that had been crushed earlier. There was debris everywhere and men trying to swim about, struggling against the waves. Everyone else drowned except for Jules Durat, who made his way to the whaleboat.

We sat arm in arm all day and night on the boat bench submerged to our necks. If sharks came around, we slapped the water to chase them away. They weren't hungry because they had thirty drowned men to choose from.

Hungry, thirsty, and cold, the two men somehow managed to catch a live crab and eat it. But after two days, they gave up all hope of being rescued. Then, on the fourth day, they spied what Degrasse at first thought was a cloud on the horizon. It was the *Fred W. Thurber.*

Since we couldn't move, we had to have ropes put around us and then were hoisted aboard ship. We were so crippled and frozen that they had to pry us apart.

The captain kept us in his cabin for the first few days because he knew we'd ask the crew members for water. We were so thirsty, and drinking water would have killed us. He had to spoon feed us warm milk and water, a teaspoon at a time, until we gained our strength.

The *Fred W. Thurber* safely brought Degrasse and Durat to New Bedford. Degrasse never set foot again on board a ship. Years later, a Hollywood director asked him to play a small part in a movie he was filming called *Moby Dick*. All Degrasse had to do was jump overboard from a ship. "He offered to pay me $125 per month. I said, "Look, Mister, you could pay me a thousand dollars, but I'm not going to jump overboard from any boat." And he didn't.

Besides the danger of rough weather, accidents were common during a voyage. A man might fall from the masthead to the deck or slice his fingers on the swordlike boarding knife or, while stowing the barrels below, be crushed under a cask holding 350 gallons (1,325 liters) of whale oil.

Robert Cushman Murphy

It was a terrific opportunity for Robert Cushman Murphy, who had recently graduated from college. He could ship aboard the *Daisy* as assistant navigator on a one-year voyage and experience first-hand the business of whaling. What he didn't realize was that his voyage would also teach him about the care and companionship crew members developed for each other. He wrote about that relationship in his diary during his voyage. More than thirty years later, he published his diary as a book called *Logbook for Daisy*.

Ferleão, whom I now see daily, is going out like the last flickers from the wick of a whale-oil lamp. He seems completely listless and at peace. The tenderness and consideration of his shipmates is a revelation of man's innate mercy. They know that he has only days to live. Their role and responsibility are something quite apart from the quarterdeck and cabin. They vie with one another, like nuns, to give him comfort. They feed him, wash him with warm water from the galley, keep him clad in clean shirt and cotton trousers, and neither balk nor gag because of vomit, blood, or excrement.

A few days later the cabin boy, Johnny, shyly approached the captain on deck with a disturbing message from the dying man below. "Ferleão, he say he going to die today."

The Old Man spit out an oath, banged the painted canvas with his fist, and told Johnny to get below and bring no more foolish messages from the forecastle. His show of temper was, however, nothing other than an attempt to rustle up a confidence which he could not feel, because as soon as the cabin boy was out of the sight, the captain turned to me and whispered weakly, "When they say they are going to die, they always do."

The Ocean Burial

On British or Canadian whaleships a doctor was usually among the ship's crew. But on American whalers the captain assumed the doctor's role. In his cabin was a chest of medicines, including syrups and Epsom salts. But when these simple medications failed and death resulted, the ship's crew gathered on deck for a most solemn ceremony—burial at sea. The captain might read a prayer. Then the body, sewn up in a canvas sack, was cast into the sea.

Samuel Morgan

Seasick during the first weeks of his voyage on the *South Boston*, Samuel Morgan, sixteen, eventually got his sea legs. In his journal he wrote about another crew member who did not recover. Joe King was dying of dropsy. Dropsy occurs when a body cannot get rid of excess fluids. It could be caused by failure of the heart, lungs, or liver, or by some severe shock to the nervous system. Whatever the cause, there was no cure.

> December 4. Joe King, who has been sick more or less since we left home, he died about 1 o'clock P.M. His disease was supposed to be dropsy. . . . it was thought he could not live but he [ate] a hearty breakfast and this morning appeared better. Towards night a strong breeze sprung up, had to shorten sail, increasing all night. At 4 A.M. called all hands to furl sail for it had arrived to a gale of wind. . . . At 9 A.M. brought the corpse aft on deck and sewed it up in canvas and put a bag of bricks at its feet and laid it on a board. Called all hands and took it in the waist. When the mate began to read a prayer, the crew were all gathered all around with their hats off. When Mr. Heath (the mate) had partly read the prayers, the signal was given and the corpse was launched forever from view in the raging ocean and when the prayer was finished the crew returned to their places not a word being spoken by any of them. But I suppose they would have felt worse had he not been a Portugee. It is customary to *haul aback the main yard* to bury a person at sea but there was danger of them being carried away. Wind not any worse, large seas tipped with white foam howling all around us, and when the ship pitched it looks more like we are sliding down from a huge mountain.

turn the sails so that they are pushed backward by the wind, slowing the ship

After the ocean burial, the crew usually auctioned off the dead man's clothing and possessions. The money they raised would be given to the man's widow or mother or some other family member once the ship returned home.

Was the ocean burial cruel? No, it was practical. A body would decay long before the ship could reach home. And while officers or members of the captain's family might be preserved in a cask of alcohol as Shuman Gray was, the common sailors were buried at sea or, if land was near enough, buried on some foreign land. The business of whaling could not stop because of the death of one man or one woman.

After a body plunged into the cold water, the ship might pass over the spot once or twice, and then sail away. The search for Neptune's giants went on.

Through all this month I have been very comfortable; though very cold, and the ship has been covered with ice; the fog congealed to the rigging, and every rope encased in an icy tube . . . The men have looked very solemn, having neither danced nor sung. They can have no fire, and it's a mystery to me how they can keep from freezing.
Clara Wheldon

The Loss of the Arctic Fleet

Whalers were explorers. But most did not want to be. They didn't care about discovering new islands or exploring unknown oceans. They wanted only to fill the ship's hold with oil and bone as quickly as possible, then return home again. But hunting Neptune's giants meant following the whales into waters where no other ships would go.

By 1776, the whaleships from Nantucket had discovered the rich ocean pastures off the western coast of Africa and off the Falkland Islands in the South Atlantic Ocean. By 1792, American whaleships had sailed around treacherous Cape Horn at the southern tip of South America, crossing from the Atlantic into the Pacific Ocean. Other whaleships soon followed, and in the 1800s the Sandwich Islands (present-day Hawaii) became an important stopover for the hundreds of whaleships that now made up the Pacific fleet. From there, the ships followed Neptune's giants to the waters off Australia and Japan. But whales were becoming scarcer. Then, in July 1848, the *Superior* became the first American whaleship to venture into the ice-clotted sea at the top of the world—the Arctic Ocean.

The Bering Strait is a ribbon of shallow seawater, 50 miles (80 kilometers) wide, between Russia and Alaska. It was through this narrow passage that the *Superior* sailed to reach the mysterious waters of the Arctic Ocean. There on all sides stretched a weird landscape of ice fields. But more important, in the ice-caked sea beneath the *Superior* were herds of whales.

These whales were different from the others the *Superior* had hunted. They were bowheads, a type of right whale. Like all other right whales, the bowhead had curtains of baleen in its mouth, but the baleen was much longer and therefore more valuable. The bowheads were different in another important way—a single cow could yield an incredible 120 barrels (455 liters) of oil, more than twice the oil of a single sperm whale!

The *Superior* had made a golden discovery. The ship pushed farther north into the Arctic, easily taking whale after whale. When at last its hold was filled with barrels of oil, the ship returned to Honolulu with the news of its discovery of a new hunting ground. Captains from all over the Pacific headed north. Within two years, more than 200 whaleships had turned the Arctic Ocean into a killing field. More than 1,700 bowheads were harpooned during the summer of 1850 alone.

Hunting in the ice meant taking new risks. Arctic ice is sometimes solid but at times it shifts. Wind and ocean currents push and pile the ice packs together. Like crazy building blocks the size of houses with sharp angles and peaks, icebergs could grind and chew a ship's hull and send it to the bottom of the ocean in a few hours.

A Warning

Native people, including Inuit, who lived along the shores of this frozen land had been hunting the bowheads for generations. They hunted in walrus-skin canoes called umiaks. They killed whales for food and took only what they needed to survive. But commercial whaleships killed as many whales as possible, not for survival—for money. Four years after the *Superior*'s cruise into the Arctic, so many bowheads had been slaughtered that the mammals were becoming scarce. One captain wrote a letter warning the whaling industry that the bowhead population would become extinct if the whaleships continued to hunt in the Arctic. The letter was published anonymously in the *Whaleman's Shipping List and Merchants' Transcript*, a newspaper read by captains and ship owners.

Letter from the Arctic

At Sea, December 22, 1852

I spoke in my last [letter] of the fact that, while at first the polar whale was most easily captured, his nature had been entirely changed by constant and untiring pursuit. He is no longer the slow and sluggish beast we at first found him. . . .

I know the whales have diminished since I was here two years ago and they are more difficult to strike. How can it be otherwise? Look at the immense fleet, stretching from Cape Thaddeus to the Straits! By day and night, the whale is chased and harassed—the fleet perpetually driving them, until they reach the highest navigable latitudes of the Arctic. The only rest they have is when the fogs are thick and the wind is high. . . .

If the ships were to withdraw for ten years, you might again have good whaling. Would it not be the wisest course to pursue?

The author's advice went unheeded. The killing continued. Then, in 1871, a strange twist of fate changed everything.

The Hunters Become the Hunted

Wind and sails, weather and whales—four important elements in navigating a whaleship—turned against the Arctic fleet in the summer of 1871. Because so many bowheads had been killed in previous years, ships risked sailing farther north and staying longer in the Arctic waters in order to fill their holds. On August 29, a gale rose. The wind gusted from the southwest. House-size blocks of ice ground toward shore. Within days, 32 ships and more than a thousand men, women, and children were stranded in a channel of water a half-mile (0.8 kilometer) wide and only 24 feet (7 meters) deep. The fleet simply had nowhere to go.

Remarks Aboard the Henry Taber

It is likely that either the captain or the first mate of the *Henry Taber* penned the journal entry below, describing the Arctic disaster as it occurred.

smashed (had a hole made in her hull)

Friday, September 1st. This day begins with moderate breeze from the S W. At 7 O'clock the bark *Roman* was crushed in the ice and at 7 O'clock P.M. a part of the officers & crew came on board of me. She was *stove* a little S of the Seahorse Islands in 5 minutes after the ice struck. Her masts went over the side and she went

The Arctic Fleet hemmed in by ice. The loss
of this fleet in 1871 proved to be a disaster
for the American whaling industry.

rear

down *stern* first. All hands took to their boats. 9 O'clock wind from the N W. So ends this day.

The wind did not change. The bergs ground toward shore. The hunters had become the hunted.

two-masted whaler

Saturday, September 2d. This day begins with light winds from the N. At 4 O'clock the *brig Comet* set a signal of distress & I ran on the ice & went to her assistance. At 5 O'clock the ice crushed her sides in & the crew abandoned her & she was sold at auction to the highest bidder. She & all her effects sold for the sum of thirteen dollars. We were tied to the same peak of ice that the brig was. At 9 O'clock A.M. we cast off from the ice & went one mile or so S W then anchored. The captain of the brig came on board of us to stay.
So ends this day.

A rescue fleet was 60 miles (97 kilometers) to the south, beyond Icy Cape. But to reach those ships, the men, women, and children would have to travel in the whaleboats through the narrow slices of open water. Ice could just as easily shatter those smaller vessels, too.

If the crews abandoned the ships, they would have to leave behind the hundreds of pounds of whalebone and thousands of barrels of oil already taken, a harvest worth more than a million dollars to the owners. But if they stayed with the ships, they risked being crushed in the ice.

It was a life-and-death decision. Finally, the captains agreed. They would abandon their ships and all the valuable cargo.

William Earle William Earle was first mate on the *Emily Morgan*. His journal—but not his ship—survived the ice. In it, he described the fleet's desperate escape.

> Sept. 9. . . . The sea off shore is one vast expanse of ice, not a speck of water to be seen in that direction. All but three of the Northern fleet have come down and anchored near us. There are twenty-one ships of us being close together. There seems to be but little hope of our saving the ship or any of the other ships being saved.
>
> Sept. 14. . . . Called all hands at 5 A.M., had breakfast and commenced loading the boats as all hope of saving ship or property is gone. If we save our lives, we ought to be satisfied and that should satisfy the world. To winter here might be possible, but not under present circumstances. We have neither the clothes nor the provisions, so to remain would entail an amount of suffering from cold and hunger and loss of life as would not justify anyone in attempting *let out* it. At twelve noon, *paid out* all of chain on both anchors and at 1:30 P.M., with sad hearts, ordered all the men into the boats and with a last look over the deck, abandoned the ship to the mercy of the elements. And so ends this day, the writer having done his duty and believes every man to have done the same.

A fugitive fleet of hundreds of whaleboats began the 60-mile (97-kilometer) journey, feeling its way through thick fog and blowing snow. William Earle described the destruction he witnessed as he and the others continued to struggle south.

> All the ships we passed were abandoned or their crews leaving in their boats. Hundreds of boats were ahead of us, as far as the eye

could search. The last vessel we passed was the brig *Victoria* of San Francisco, hard aground and being well over on her side.

. . . As night came on, the wind increased and as darkness closed around us heavy, black clouds seemed to rest over us and it was not possible to see more than a few feet and we were in constant danger of coming in collision with the many fragments of ice floating in the narrow passage between the land and the main pack.

At 10:30 P.M., landed by a fire on the shore, where several boats were hauled up and made some coffee. While we were on shore, the wind began to increase, with some rain. . . . Shoved off into the darkness at 11:30. The navigation was difficult and dangerous.

The fresh breeze lasted till about 1:30 A.M., with a darkness almost black. Just as the wind began to die away, one of our boats *breaking* came in contact with a small piece of ice, *staving* a hole in her bows. She hauled up on the beach and the hole being fortunately above water, soon repaired and followed.

Morning found Earle and three other whaleboats still 20 miles (32 kilometers) northeast of Icy Cape. They had navigated the narrow channel of open water all night. Now they beached their boats on the ice to rest a while and drink hot coffee. But they could not linger long, for the wind was rising. Exhausted, they climbed aboard and shoved off again.

sailing in a zigzag into the wind

Continuing along the land to SW of the Cape, which we did by beating, *tacking* and with oars between the ice and land till six or seven miles to South of the Cape, when we took dinner at 3 P.M. on a long fragment of ice. After some search, found an opening in the ice and with a fair wind, delivered the whole crew of the *Emily Morgan* on board of the ship *Europa* of Edgartown safely.

Incredibly, not one whaleboat or life was lost. But the million-dollar-cargo as well as thirty-two ships were gone. The loss would speed up the decline of the American whaling industry.

"He's dead, Mr. Stubb."
"Yes; both pipes smoked out!" and withdrawing his own from his mouth, Stubb scattered the dead ashes over the water; and for a moment, stood thoughtfully eyeing the vast corpse he had made.

Herman Melville, Moby Dick

The Hunt

Illness, mistreatment, treacherous seas—whalemen endured these and other hardships for one reason: to hunt whales. Crisscrossing oceans for months at a time, whiling away the weeks at tedious tasks, perhaps some could forget this fact. But, if so, such forgetting faded fast.

Songs from the Mast

"There she blows!"
This and similar "songs" from the masthead quickly reminded men of their mission. On a whaler, lookouts were sent to watch from the masthead about 100 feet (30 meters) above the deck. From this point, sailors took turns keeping "a weather eye" over the ocean for the sudden spout of a whale. When they spotted the fountain of warm breath, they called the news to their mates below: "There she blows!"

Nelson Cole Haley

Seventeen-year-old Nelson Haley was aboard the *Charles W. Morgan* when the lookout summoned him. In his book *Whale Hunt*, Haley described the amazing sight of whales at play.

We had just finished supper and lit our pipes, when the man at the masthead sung out:

"School of sperm whales on the *lee beam* not half a mile off!"

side of ship away from wind

Casting our eyes in that direction, we could see twenty or thirty good-sized whales tumbling about when the big seas would catch them and almost turn them over. Sometimes one could be seen on the crest of a wave. As it broke he would shoot down its side with such speed a streak of white could be seen in the wake he made through the water. When reaching the hollow between seas he would lazily shove his spout holes above the water and blow out his spout, as much as to say, "See how that is done." I have never seen whales at play before or since. It seemed too bad to interrupt their pastime, but they were the fish we had crossed three oceans and into the fourth to find.

Once a whale was spotted, the crew sprang into action. The *Morgan*, like all whalers, was equipped with davits. These arched supports held the smaller whaleboats from which whales were actually hunted. Whaleboats were sleek and fast and could pursue whales for hours, even days. Within minutes of a sighting, a crew lowered the craft from the davits. Harpooners, oarsmen, and officers climbed aboard and the chase was on.

Striking and Sounding

The weapons of the hunt included the harpoon and the lance. The harpoon was an iron shaft with a barbed head attached to a long wooden handle. It was the boatsteerer's task to plant, not throw, the harpoon solidly into the whale's back so that the sharp barbs stuck. This was called "getting fast." The lance was like a spear and was used for striking the whale at close distance.

Robert Cushman Murphy took this picture of men on the *Daisy*'s masthead about 1913. When one of these men shouted, "There she blows!" the crew sprang into action.

The whale might react to this attack by sounding, diving deep below the surface. As the whale fled, the rope attached to the harpoon whirled out of the boat. One hundred, 200, 300 feet (30, 60, 90 meters) of line followed the whale into the water. At other times, the fleeing giant often whipped the whaleboat and the men in it over the ocean waves.

Nelson Cole Haley

Haley boarded one of the *Morgan's* whaleboats on the rolling waves. He remembered what the ship's owner, Black Hawk Robinson, and the captain had asked him that day while the ship was still in port: "Do you think you can strike a whale?" This, finally, was Haley's moment of truth.

rowing

After *pulling* before the wind and sea a short time, I looked over my shoulder ahead of the boat, and as the boat rose I could see the whales tumbling and rolling no great distance off. By the way we were shooting over the water, not many minutes more would elapse before I should have passed through my trial, and be honored, or *demoted* disgraced, as a boatsteerer; and, if failing, I would be *disrated,* sent *before the mast* *forward,* and never more have a chance to become above the common sailor on board a whale ship. These thoughts went through my mind, and although I did not fear a whale it made me nervous, as this would be the first time for me to strike one. . . .

As we got on top of a big sea, the 2d Mate sternly sang out to me: "Stand up!"

lifting; harpoon *Peaking* my oar, jumping to my feet, grasping the first *iron* in my hands, mind made up to do or die, I saw three whales right ahead. *between waves* I was looking down at them as they lay *in the hollow* of the sea, and could make out every part of their upper sides and plainly see their

During the chase, boatsteerers prepare to plunge
lances into a sperm whale in this 1859 lithograph.

big flukes in motion as they slowly twisted them from side to side. They . . . [were] unaware of the sharp cruel iron that would soon penetrate one of their sides. I had hardly time to brace myself firmly against the *clumsy cleat* when the boat shot down the side of the sea, and amid the roar of breaking water with the boat's head a few feet clear of the whale, I darted first one iron and then the other *chock to the hitches,* just forward his hump.

Never in my life have I had such feelings of relief and pleasure, as I saw the line run out when the whale dove into the depths, drawing it after him. . . . I had struck my first whale and proved that a boy only seventeen years old could fill a man's place on a whale man's deck.

notch in boat's bow for the harpooner's thigh

all the way in

Stoved!

Once their prey had sounded, the crew of a whaleboat could do nothing but hang on and wait for the whale to tire. Eventually, the exhausted animal stopped running. The men then began to haul in the line, drawing closer and closer to the wounded whale. Often the men beached the boat right on the whale's slippery back. This dangerous maneuver was called "bringing wood to black skin."

On sperm whale hunts, violent confrontations often came with these phases of the hunt. Unlike the right whale, a sperm whale has no baleen. Along its lower jaw are huge pegs of ivory teeth. These teeth aren't used for chewing, but for fighting. At least, that is what many scientists think, and what many whalers experienced to be true. When attacked, a sperm whale often fought back, snapping its jaws and smacking its massive flukes on the water.

"A dead whale or a stove boat" was a saying whalemen used to describe the life-and-death tugs of war they fought—and sometimes lost—on the oceans. A stove boat was a smashed boat. A crash of the whale's powerful flukes or a snap of its jaws could send the men somersaulting into the air.

Most men and women who kept journals during a whaling voyage did not write with the hope that one day their books would be published and read by strangers. Their journals were mostly a record of the voyage.

Once they returned home, their journals might be shared with family members or friends, then tucked away in a drawer or a sea chest. That was not the case with Frank Bullen.

Frank Bullen

In 1899, Bullen wrote and published a book called *The Cruise of the Chachalot.* Chachalot is the French word for sperm whale. It was also, according to Bullen, the name of the whaling vessel on which he had shipped.

His book was not a whaling log or journal. It read, in fact, more like a novel with many exciting, even melodramatic, scenes. Perhaps Bullen's *Chachalot,* like George H. Newton's Prince of Whales exhibit, was a hyped-up show meant to please an American public that was hungry for suspenseful adventure stories. Still, the book includes some valuable information about whaling.

In this scene from Bullen's book, a sperm whale is in a violent fury as it fights to free itself from the hunters and their harpoons. Even though the writing is dramatic, being stoved by a whale was a real danger that all whalemen faced.

Whales sometimes fought back before they were captured, thrashing the water with their mighty flukes and, perhaps, overturning the whaleboat.

straight against

bottom

openings; throat

confusion

knot

I saw his tail, like a vast shadow, sweeping away from us towards the second mate, who was laying off the other side of him. Before I had time to think, the mighty mass of gristle leapt into the sunshine, curved back from us like a huge bow. Then with a roar it came at us, released from its tension of Heaven knows how many tons. *Full on the broadside* it struck us, sending every soul but me flying out of the wreckage as if fired from catapults. I did not go because my foot was jammed somehow in the *well* of the boat, but the wrench nearly pulled my thigh-bone out of its socket. I had hardly released my foot, when, towering above me, came the colossal head of the great creature, as he ploughed through the bundle of debris that had just been a boat. There was an appalling roar of water in my ears, and darkness that might be felt all around. Yet, in the midst of it all, one thought predominated as clearly as if I had been turning it over in my mind in the quiet of my bunk aboard—"What if he should swallow me?" Nor to this day can I understand how I escaped the *portals* of his *gullet*, which of course gaped wide as a church door. But the agony of holding my breath soon overpowered every other feeling and thought, till just as something was going to snap inside my head, I rose to the surface. I was surrounded by a *welter* of bloody froth, which made it impossible for me to see; but oh, the air was sweet!

I struck out blindly. . . . My hand touched and clung to a rope, which immediately towed me in some direction—I neither knew nor cared whither. Soon the motion ceased, and, with a seaman's instinct, I began to haul myself along by the rope I grasped, attached. Presently I came butt up against something solid, the feel of which gathered all my scattered wits into a compact *knub* of dread. It was the whale!

Bullen's whale was in its final struggle, which the whalemen called "the death flurry." Its death flurry involved swimming in wild circles until it eventually slowed, rolled on its side, and died.

Chimney Afire!

Although sailors sometimes perished in such contests, whales lost the vast number of times. Once a whaleboat was close enough to a whale, the death blow was struck. Using the lance, the officer or the captain repeatedly stabbed a spot behind the whale's neck where the arteries—blood vessels leading away from the heart—collected near the lungs. The whale suffocated in its own blood. Now, instead of spouting air and foam from its blow hole, the dying whale sent up a column of clotted blood. Whales in such mortal condition were said by sailors to have their "chimneys afire."

Robert Cushman Murphy

Robert Murphy sailed in the twilight days of whaling in 1912. Although his boat's officer used a hand-held lance, by then gun-fired bomb lances were employed as well. No matter what the weapon, Murphy's whale—like tens of thousands of Neptune's giants during American whaling—fought a losing battle for survival.

group

The turning point of the struggle came when the frantic whale once more fell in with a *gam* of his fellows. The calming influence was soon apparent, for he allowed us to draw right toward him. We pulled ourselves through an acre of sperm whales, big bulls that we might have touched with oars, cows at arm's length, and tiny calves, ten or twelve feet long, with huge *remoras* clinging to their flanks.

fish with suction disks

The crew of the whaleboat placed
their craft on the animal itself to
better strike the killing blow.

don't so much as move the chewing tobacco in your mouth

"Shush, easy, easy boys!" whispered Mr. da Lomba [the mate]; "trim the boat; *don't shift your quids.*"

We hauled softly along the length of another whale and, when our line was as short as a dog leash, the mate braced his thigh in the clumsy cleat, raised his long powerful arms, and buried the five-foot shank of the lance in blubber and flesh. The tortured whale quivered and sank. We peered tensely over the side for his dark hulk, knowing that the sounding would be brief and that he must rise beneath us.

Murphy did not have long to wait. The whale soon surfaced for the final time.

clotted with blood

His spout, formerly so thin and white, reflecting tiny rainbows in the rays of the low sun, now became first pink and then crimson and *gouted.*

"His chimney's afire!" said Mr. da Lomba with a heartless chuckle.

Mr. Almeida's boat closed in with ours. Lances were thrust between the whale's ribs, held there, and churned, until the creature went into his ghastly flurry, all the while belching squids from his gullet until we floated in a slimy pool of their remains.

He died and turned fin out after giving us nine thrilling hours. We chopped a hole though one of his flukes, attached a line, and rested, weary but content, munching hard bread, drinking fresh water, and awaiting the arrival of the distant brig which, happily, was then to *windward.* After all the bluster of the day, the sun set in a calm sky.

toward the wind

CHAPTER SIX

The Floating Factory

One time we had four whales along-side, but you cut them all in before you stop to eat. You start cutting in and you don't stop no 12 o'clock, no one o'clock for dinner, you keep going until you cut that entire whale in and then you can eat again.
Charles A. Arnaud

The whale was dead. Now the dirty work began.

Towing the giant to the ship was a back-breaking task that often took hours. One boat, six men, and twelve arms fought the wind and the waves and the dead weight of the whale. Often the sun set long before the men could get their prize back to the ship. Then the captain ordered lanterns hung in the rigging to guide the men back safely.

When at last the carcass was alongside the ship, every man, from the foremast hand to the captain, soon was at work. The ship became a floating factory.

Cutting In, Trying Out

A whale was much too large to haul onto the deck, at least not in one piece. Instead, the men worked on a wooden platform called a cutting stage, which was lowered over the side of the ship. The narrow planks were only a few feet above the rolling water and the snapping jaws of sharks that were drawn to the carcass by the trail of blood.

Eliza Williams

Eliza Williams sailed with her husband, the captain of the *Florida*. Her curiosity about the whales drew her from the captain's cabin onto the deck where she could watch the men cutting in the whale. Cutting in meant stripping off the blubber in long pieces. Author Herman Melville compared the process to peeling a rind from an orange. In her journal, parts of which were published later in the book *One Whaling Family*, Williams describes the process:

tied up to the main mast; pulleys

It must be quite an art, as well as a good deal of work, to cut in the whale. He is all the time lying on the surface of the water as they work at him. He is made secure in the position they want him, at first, lying close alongside of the ship. A Man goes right down on his back, and hooks a large stout hook into a rope that is made fast to his jaw. This is *made fast up* by means of ropes and *tackles*. They have two stagings let down at the side of the Ship. The Men go down and stand on these, with their long spades, and cut. They seem to know exactly where to cut. They begin to cut a great strip. The hook is put through a hole that is cut in the end of this piece by the boarding knife. Then it is drawn up by the tackle as they cut. They do not stop till the piece goes clear around. Then it comes clear up and is let down into the blubber room where it is afterwards cut in pieces suitable for the mincing machine. They keep cutting in that way till it is all off; even the flukes and fins have a good deal of fat on them. The head they cut off and take on

amazing

board in the same way that the rest is. It was *singular* to me to see how well they could part the head from the body and find the joint so nicely. When it came on deck, it was such a large head, it swung against the side of the Ship till it seemed to me to shake with the weight of it.

These are samples of the implements used by whaling crew members. Sailors who were not injured during the struggle to capture the whale could easily be hurt by the careless use of these tools.

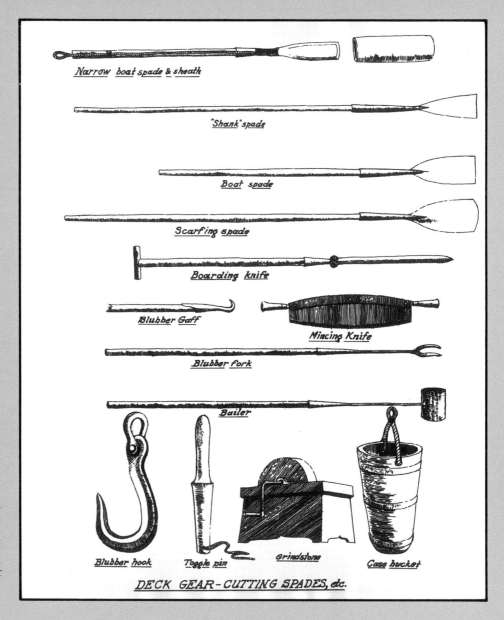

Narrow boat spade & sheath

"Shank" spade

Boat spade

Scarfing spade

Boarding knife

Blubber Gaff

Mincing Knife

Blubber fork

Bailer

Blubber hook   Toggle pin   Grindstone   Case bucket

DECK GEAR–CUTTING SPADES, etc.

It was all done and I was glad for the Men, for it seemed to me that they must be very tired, and such a bad place for them to work. It made me tremble to see them stand there on that narrow staging, with a rope passed around their bodies and made fast to the Ship to keep them from going over, while they leaned forward to cut. Every Man was at work, from the foremast hand to the Captain. The sharks were around the Ship and I saw one fellow, more bold than the rest, I suppose, almost to the whale to get a bite. The huge carcass floated away, and they had it all to themselves.

To retrieve all the spermaceti oil, a man might climb inside the whale's head. Often he stood up to his armpits in oil, scooping out buckets of the stuff. With that task completed, the crew cut off the lips and tongue and removed the giant pegs of ivory from the jaw bone. Then the head was heaved over the side of the ship. It sank quickly, teasing the sharks that tore after it.

One morning after still another whale had been brought along-side the ship, Eliza Williams gave in to her curiosity.

December 4th. This morning the Men were up as soon as they could see to work, cutting in the whale. . . . I went up on deck when they were hoisting the head up. It certainly is a great curiosity. How can I describe it? It seems to me I should want to examine it for a week to give a correct opinion of it.

I could not stay up but a few minutes, it rained so very hard. My husband wanted me to walk into the whale's mouth. He pushed me in a little ways, so I think I can say that I have been inside of a whale's mouth. Six or eight people could easily go in and sit down at one time. I would not hesitate about going in and sitting down if it was clean, but it was very wet and dirty from the rain. . . .

The blubber room was a compartment between the decks. Here the men hacked the thick blankets of blubber into smaller pieces. Always curious, Eliza Williams one day got a good look at what went on in the blubber room.

> In the afternoon, the mate came to me and wanted me to go with him and take a look down in the reception room, as he termed it. I went, and I could not refrain from laughter, such a comical sight! There the men were at work up to their waists in blubber. The *melted* warm weather had *tried out* the oil a good deal and made it soft. I don't see how they could stand in among it, but they were laughing and having a good deal of fun. I had heard the Men tell about the blubber room, but I had not had the pleasure of seeing it before.

Once all the blanket pieces had been minced into small sections that looked similar to a book with pages of sliced blubber, they were tried out.

Trying out meant boiling the blubber into oil. A whaleship had on its deck a brick oven with huge iron pots called a tryworks. Flames from the furnace cast a glow over the ship as men used long-handled skimmers to remove the burnt scraps of fat. When the oil cooled, the men poured it into barrels and stowed them below.

Eliza Williams noted:

> That odor with the smoke that comes below from the tryworks is quite unpleasant, but I can bear it all first rate when I consider that it is filling our ship all the time and by and by it will all be over and we will go home.

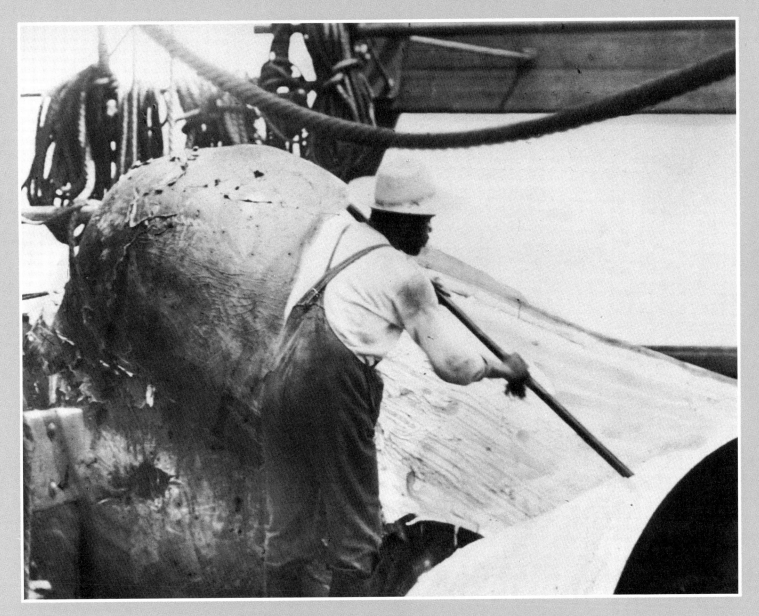

A sailor "cutting in" to a whale: stripping off blubber in sheets so it could be boiled into precious oil.

And indeed, the *Florida* did head for home, like many whaleships, with its hold full of the oil of Neptune's hunted giants. This final crossing of the oceans could take months. But as home finally loomed closer on the horizon, the crew took apart the brick tryworks and happily heaved the bricks into the sea. This officially signaled the end of a journey. "We are making sacrifices to Neptune this morning," wrote Adra Ashley, a whaling wife on the *Reindeer*, "throwing the tryworks overboard, which says good-bye to whaling."

As the ship slowly made its way into its home port, it was often in need of repairs. Two or three years of slashing winds and salt spray had resulted in patched sails, which were no longer white but stained a tarry brown from days and nights of boiling blubber on deck. The ship's hull wore a coat of crusty barnacles and moss. Hidden beneath that sea jacket might be ship worms that had bored into the bottom, causing leaks.

But within a few weeks, a transformation began to take place. The treasured whalebone and barrels of oil were unloaded on the dock and covered with seaweed. New sails and ropes replaced the oil. The ship's hull was scraped and new copper sheets nailed to her bottom. The whaler was ready, once more, to go hunting.

The voyages continued, again and again, until at last, the demand for whale oil and bone was no more.

The Princess

A dying whale turned fin out and faced the sun. Or so the whalemen said. In the early twentieth century it was the American whaling industry that turned fin out. Its death flurry had lasted more than fifty years.

In 1846, 735 American whaleships hunted the oceans. By 1906, only 42 whaleships remained. Why?

The discovery of petroleum oil in Pennsylvania in 1859 and the use of other sources of fuel—coal and kerosene—were like harpoons planted in the back of the American whaling industry. Like the struck whale, the industry fought to stay alive. But the sinking of Yankee whaleships during the Civil War and the loss of the Arctic Fleet in 1871 were the lance that pierced the heart of the industry—its profits.

Yes, right whales, sperm whales, and now bowheads were scarce, almost to the point of extinction. But it was the loss of profits that was the death blow to American whaling. It was for money that the Quakers of Nantucket first launched their whaleships. When large amounts of money could no longer be made from killing whales, the ship owners gave up whaling and invested in other businesses—factories, farms, mines. In harbors and ports along the New England coast, the wooden ribs of whaleships lay rotting in the sun or were towed to scrap yards to be burned.

The International Whaling Commission

For centuries, there were no rules or laws to govern whaling. Any country could kill as many whales as it wanted. No one was going to stop it. Whales were simply there for the taking.

In the 1920s, however, a change began to occur. The first country to protect whales from the hunt was not America but Norway. In 1929, the Norwegians wrote a law called the Norwegian Whaling Act. It said that no right whales could be captured. Females and calves of *all* species, and blue whales less than 60 feet (18 meters) in length could not be killed, either.

In 1945, the International Whaling Commission formed and held its first meeting in Washington, D.C., to discuss what should be done to protect whales. The American deep-sea whaling industry had come to an end, but countries like Japan and the former Soviet Union still hunted whales. Norwegian law did not rule them. And so the pursuit continued. After World War II, commercial whalers—those who killed whales for profit—began to use new electronic equipment to turn the hunt even more in their favor. Airplanes spotted whales from the sky. Pilots radioed the whales' locations to ships' captains. Radar locked onto the submerged whales to track them as they swam. When a whale surfaced, a whaleship was there, waiting. It was no longer necessary for a crew

Whaling ships as they appeared
when the American whaling industry was at its height.

to risk their lives by bringing wood to black skin. The cannon-fired harpoon could strike and kill a whale from a safe distance.

And so whales continued to die. In 1968 alone, more than 15,000 sperm whales were killed. It wasn't until 1982 that the International Whaling Commission, which now included thirty-seven countries, passed an accord, or agreement, forbidding all commercial whaling. There would be no more killing for profit.

The ban did much to protect whales, but agreements are difficult to enforce. As this book was being written, the hunt for whale oil and bone was still going on.

The Cruise of the *Portuguese Princess*

The fog is lifting. The horizon is still pink with dawn. On a wharf in Provincetown, Massachusetts, the people shiver as they wait in line to board the *Portuguese Princess*. It is May, but still cold this far north along the coast of the Atlantic Ocean.

The boat's propellers churn the water, engines idling. On this vessel there are no mastheads, davits, or tryworks; no forecastle or hold; no harpoons, lances, or cutting spades. And yet the *Portuguese Princess* is a hunter of whales. The people waiting in line are now allowed to board. Within minutes, the deck is filled and the *Princess* is under way.

The ride is rough. The boat bounces out of the bay and into the ocean. An hour passes, then two. All eyes on deck squint across the steely water, hoping to spy the warm spray of breath from a finback or humpback whale. "There!" a woman cries and points. All eyes turn. The black flukes of a finback slip gracefully below the surface as the whale sounds.

Now the impatient waiting begins. The passengers know the whale can't stay below forever. It must surface again to breathe. And it does, blowing its spout as if to say, "See, that is how it is done."

The *Portuguese Princess* does not give chase. Laws now require that boats keep a safe distance from whales. But the boat keeps pace with the finback, and those on deck lift their cameras, take aim, and shoot.

George H. Newton would have liked this whale show. "Those seeking knowledge must see it!" he might cry. "If you love your children, don't deny them the only opportunity they may ever have in their lives to see this Monarch of the seas!"

This Prince of Whales is not dead. It rises to the surface. Its sleek, black back glistens in the sun that has just broken through the clouds. The whale blows, turns flukes up, and sounds again, slipping silently out of sight—alive.

Sources

Arnaud, Charles A., oral history collection, George W. Blunt White Library, Mystic Seaport Museum (hereafter GWBWL).

Braley, Capt. Samuel, as quoted in Miller, Pamela A. *And the Whale Is Ours.* (Boston: David R. Godine, in association with The Kendall Whaling Museum, Sharon, Mass., 1979).

Bullen, Frank T. *The Cruise of the Cachalot.* (New York: Dover Publishing Inc., 1962). Original book was published in 1899.

Chippendale, Harry Alan. *Sails and Whales.* (Cambridge, MA: The Riverside Press, 1951).

Corvello, Roderick, as quoted in "Tales of Twentieth Century Whaling," *Spinner: People and Culture in Southeastern Massachusetts,* Volume 2. (New Bedford, MA: Spinner Publishers, 1982).

Degrasse, Quinton, as quoted in "Tales of Twentieth Century Whaling," *Spinner: People and Culture in Southeastern Massachusetts,* Volume 2. (New Bedford, MA: Spinner Publishers, 1982).

Earle, William, Log, New Bedford Whaling Museum and the Melville Whaling Room, New Bedford Public Library, New Bedford, MA. (Roll #23)

Fenton, Lilian Baker, VFM 1118, GWBWL.

Green, Henry, Log 201, GWBWL.

Haley, Nelson Cole. *Whale Hunt: The Narrative of a Voyage by Nelson Cole Haley, Harpooner in the Ship* Charles W. Morgan *1849–1853.* (Mystic, CT: Mystic Seaport Museum, 1990).

"Letter from the Arctic," *Whalemen's Shipping List and Merchants' Transcript, 1852,* as quoted in Allen, *Children of the Light* (Boston: Little, Brown, 1973).

Morgan, Nathanial Saxton, Log 862, GWBWL.

Morgan, Samuel B., Log 761, Old Darmouth Historical Society Whaling Museum (hereafter ODHSWM), New Bedford, MA.

Murphy, Robert Cushman. *A Dead Whale or a Stove Boat.* (Boston: Houghton Mifflin Co., 1967).

———. *Logbook for* Daisy. (New York: Macmillan Co., 1947).

Olmstead, Francis. *Incidents of a Whaling Voyage.* (Rutland, VT: Charles E. Tuttle Co., 1969). Originally published in 1841 by S. Appleton and Co., NY.

Remarks aboard the *Henry Taber,* from ship's log, ODHSWM.

States, John A., Log 69, GWBWL

Stetson, Charlie, Microfilm 176, GWBWL.

Stetson, Elizabeth, Microfilm 176, GWBWL.

Williams, Eliza, "Whaling Wife," *American Heritage,* Vol. 15:4, June 1964.

Wheldon, Clara, Log, ODHSWM.

Woods, William H., Letter, ODHSWM.

Further Information

Allen, Everett S. *Children of the Light*. Boston: Little, Brown, 1973.

Beane, Joshua Fillbrown. *From Forecastle to Cabin*. New York: The Editor Publishing Co., 1905.

Brockstoce, John R. *Whales, Ice, & Men: The History of Whaling in the Western Arctic*. Seattle: University of Washington Press in association with the New Bedford Whaling Museum, 1986.

Busch, Briton Cooper. "Whaling Will Never Do for Me". In *The American Whaleman in the Nineteenth Century*. Lexington: University Press of Kentucky, 1994.

Cohn, Michael, and Michael K. H. Platzer. *Black Men of the Sea*. New York: Dodd, Mead & Co., 1978.

Druett, Joan. *Petticoat Whalers: Whaling Wives at Sea, 1820–1920*. New Zealand: Collins Publishing, 1991.

Ellis, Richard. *Men and Whales*. New York: Alfred A. Knopf, 1991.

Hohman, Elmo P. *The American Whaleman*. New York: Longmans, Green & Co., 1928.

Melville, Herman. *Moby Dick*. Published 1851. New York: New American Library, 1961.

Miller, Pamela A. *And the Whale Is Ours.* Boston: David R. Godine Publishing, in association with The Kendall Whaling Museum, Sharon, Mass., 1979.

Stackpole, Edouard A. *The Sea Hunters: New England Whalemen During Two Centuries 1635–1835.* New York: J. B. Lippincott, 1953.

Weir, Robert. "The Adventures of a Haunted Whaling Man," *American Heritage,* August 1977.

Whipple, A. B. C. *Yankee Whales in the South Seas.* New York: Doubleday, 1954.

Whiting, Emma Mayhew, and Henry Beetle Hough. *Whaling Wives.* Boston: Houghton Mifflin Co., 1953.

Places to Visit or Call

Cold Spring Harbor Whaling Museum, Main Street, Cold Spring Harbor, NY (516) 692-9626.

Kendall Whaling Museum, 27 Everett Street, Sharon, MA (617) 784-5642.

Mystic Seaport Museum, Mystic, CT (203) 572-0711.

National Maritime Historical Society, Peekskill, NY (914) 737-7878.

Penobscot Marine Museum, Searsport, ME (207) 548-2529.

The Rhode Island Fishermen and Whale Museum, 18 Market Square, Newport, RI (401) 849-1340.

Sag Harbor Whaling Museum, Sag Harbor, NY (516) 725-0770.

San Francisco Maritime National Historical Park, Fort Mason, San Francisco, CA (415) 556-3002.

South Street Seaport Museum, 207 Front Street, New York, NY (212) 669-9400.

The Whaling Museum, Broad Street, Nantucket, MA (508) 228-1894.

The Whaling Museum, Johnny Cake Hill, New Bedford, MA (508) 997-0046.

Index

About the Author

Catherine Gourley is the author of many stories for young adults and adults, including "The Chameleon," which was awarded Best Fiction in the children's category by the Educational Press Association of America in 1993. Her historical novel *The Courtship of Joanna* was nominated for the Jefferson Cup for historical fiction. A former high school teacher of English and Writer-in-Residence for the Texas Commission on the Arts, she is currently an editor for *Read* magazine, published by the Weekly Reader Corporation, and she is a member of The Authors Guild.

About the Museum

Mystic Seaport Museum is located along the Mystic River in Mystic, Connecticut. Visitors explore ships and boats, homes and workshops typical of whaling days, exhibit galleries, and a preservation shipyard. The Museum offers educational programs and maintains a research library, where Catherine Gourley found some of the interesting stories about whaling that appear in this book.

Since 1929, Mystic Seaport Museum has been collecting wonderful objects to tell the story of American people who lived and worked on or near the sea. The most famous of all the museum's objects is the *Charles W. Morgan,* the only wooden whaleship left in America. Visitors go aboard to see where the whalers worked, ate, and slept. Also on display are the small boats they launched to hunt the whales and the giant iron pots in which they boiled whale blubber into oil.